# NORWICH CATHEDRAL

*The Cathedral Church of the Holy and Undivided Trinity*

ABOVE: *The cathedral from the south east. In the foreground, the Deanery—Norman, medieval, Georgian.*

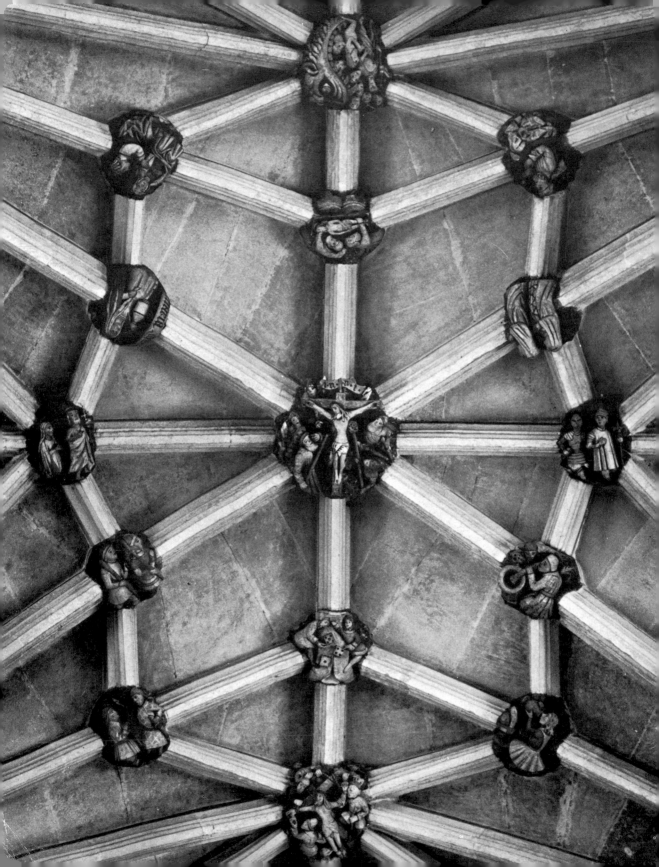

# NORWICH CATHEDRAL

## GILBERT THURLOW *

THE rarest treasure of Norwich Cathedral is a couple of ancient stones. Heavily calcined by fire, further damaged by exposure to weather for three generations, so that now they bear little resemblance to their original state, they still remain in the place of highest honour in the church, behind the High Altar.

They form all that is left of the Ancient Throne. This is the oldest bishop's throne in use in any English cathedral, and the interest of the fragments themselves is great, as is the tradition behind them.

They have recently been incorporated in a modern restoration, which follows as far as practicable the design of about 1105. The opportunity has been taken for a re-examination of them[†]. From this it appears that they were first made at least as far back as the eighth century. The See of East Anglia, fixed at Dunwich in 630 by

*

LEFT: *The bosses of the nave vault illustrate, from east to west, the Old Testament from Creation to King Solomon, then the New Testament. This picture shows the bosses in the twelfth bay from the east. From base to top, along the centre line, they depict Jesus being nailed to the Cross, the soldiers gambling for Jesus' garment, the Crucifixion, the Burial and lastly, the Harrowing of Hell.*
RIGHT: *This ancient effigy was built into a niche above the north transept door about 1100 and was moved to the ambulatory in 1968 for protection from the weather. It is possibly England's oldest Christian effigy and may represent Herbert de Losinga, Pope Gregory I, or St. Peter.*

* The author, the Very Reverend Gilbert Thurlow, M.A., F.S.A., F.R.Hist.S., Dean of Gloucester Cathedral 1973-82, was formerly Vice-Dean of Norwich Cathedral.

† See "The Bishop's Throne in Norwich Cathedral", C. A. Ralegh Radford, The Archaeological Journal, Vol CXVI, 1959, and authorities there cited.

‡ See p. 18, also Dr. Peter Wade-Martins, Norfolk Archaeology, 1969, et seq.

St. Felix, was divided into two in 673, and a cathedral, probably of timber, was built at North Elmham. It seems to have been replaced early in the eighth century by a stone cathedral, and it was probably for this cathedral that the throne was made. It would have been richly carved with scroll and perhaps with animal or bird forms, and would have stood behind the High Altar.

During the Danish invasion, about 870, Elmham Cathedral was burnt, and its throne badly damaged. The site stood neglected and open to the weather until the Bishopric was restored about 950. Then the cathedral was rebuilt, the fragments recovered, and set up again in the place of honour[‡].

After the Conquest, it was Norman policy to move bishops' sees to important cities, for the bishops' leadership was extending from the spiritual to the secular sphere. The see was therefore moved to Thetford in 1075, and the fragments of the throne were set up there. But Thetford was near Bury St. Edmunds, whose powerful abbot secured from the king and from Pope Hildebrand independence from control by the bishop. At the same time Norwich was rising in importance by reason of its position on a great estuary, so in 1095 the see was moved to Norwich. Again the fragments of the throne were moved, and set up in the new cathedral.

The tradition behind the Norwich throne goes back far beyond the eighth century—indeed to the beginning of Christianity itself. The earliest Christian worship took place in borrowed buildings. These may have included the Jewish synagogues, and the pillared halls in which the members of the Mystery cults worshipped. The influence of the Roman Law Court plan, with the judge's throne in the apse, seems clear also. A Mystery hall resembled a Roman Law Court and consisted of a hall with aisles and a semi-circular apse. Raised on steps in

the centre of the apse was the throne, with seats around it, dominating the building as the "Moses' Seat" dominated the synagogue. The description of heavenly worship in *Revelation IV* might seem to suggest a meditation in such a building, with the throne in the apse, the altar before it, the elders around it, and the "sea of glass", the mosaic pavement, forming the floor.

When Christian churches began to be built, it would be natural to follow the familiar plan. The third-century *Teaching of the Apostles* directs, "keep a place for the presbyters on the east side of the church, so that the bishop's throne may be placed among these".

When in 313 church building was made legal, this plan became general. The fifth-century *Testament of our Lord Jesus Christ* has a chapter, *How to build a church*, which says: "Let there be a throne towards the east; to the right and left places for the presbyters . . . let the place of the Throne be raised three steps for the Altar ought also to be there." This plan, known as the *Synthronus* or *Thrones together*, is a prominent feature of the earliest surviving churches. It consists of rows of seats round the apse, behind the altar, with the central seat, for the bishop, given greater importance. It can be seen in such ruined churches as those of Carthage and Jerash, and it survives in use in a number of Southern European cathedrals, such as Poreč (Istria), Ravenna, Torcello, and in Rome.

Similar thrones formed part of the normal plan of the pre-Conquest cathedrals of England. They survive at Hexham and Beverley, though no longer in apses, and with no bishops to sit on them today. By the tenth century the surrounding seats fell out of use in England; the bishop alone remained behind the altar, and when the remains were rebuilt at Elmham in 950, only one arm of the throne was re-used; the other, perhaps too much damaged, was replaced by an arm saved from the old Synthronus.

The Norwich throne remains as a unique survival in England of the primitive plan, practically universal in Christian cathedrals for several centuries. It survives here for the reason that Norwich Cathedral never produced an important saint. Almost every other cathedral did so. Now a saint needed a shrine, to accommodate which with dignity the apse must be replaced by a splendid eastward extension. So Ely had St. Etheldreda, Durham St. Cuthbert, Chichester St. Richard, and Lincoln St. Hugh, each lying in state in a glorious building. Norwich had no such magnificence, but instead it retains its ancient throne. This has recently come to have added significance, as a link between early Christian worship and the modern Liturgical Movement.

The founder of Norwich Cathedral was Herbert de Losinga. Possibly a native of Suffolk, he was educated at Fécamp, of which house he became prior. He became abbot of Ramsey, Huntingdonshire, in 1088. He was appointed by William Rufus as Bishop of Thetford in 1091. The tale is often repeated how Herbert committed simony by purchasing his preferment to the bishopric from Rufus, how he

*Continued on page 7*

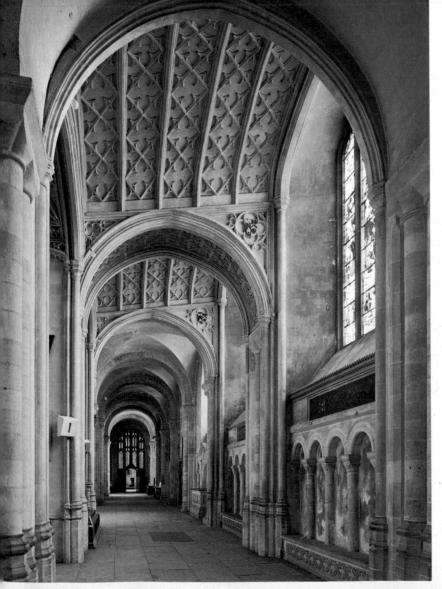

\*

LEFT: *The south nave aisle, whose modest height accentuates the impression of length. Pillars, walls and distant vaulting are Norman. Pillar bases and nearer vaulting are Perpendicular.*

RIGHT: *The nave, the people's church, looking east. The main purpose of the nave is to accommodate large numbers who come to worship in the mother church on special occasions and the processions which form a part of Christian worship.*

ABOVE: *The choir. The stalls were originally coloured. The organ case, 1950, is a fine example. The misericorde seats illustrate, underneath, various subjects, two of which are seen at left: Bishop Courtenay (1413) tending his sheep and at Oxford feeding his scholars; a monastic schoolmaster whacking a boy in the Choir School.*

★

RIGHT: *More examples (see p. 3) of roof bosses in the nave. The main central boss of each Old Testament bay appears to be a "pre-figuring" of the corresponding New Testament bays; thus, for example, bays 1 and 8, the old Adam; Christ the new Adam; 2 and 9, the flood; Christ's Baptism; 3 and 10, Abraham about to sacrifice Isaac; Christ about to consecrate the Bread; 5 and 12, Joseph in the pit; Christ crucified. The designs are simple, clear and bold.*

obtained Absolution from the pope (but not the pope whom the king recognised, for there were rival popes at the time), and founded the cathedral as a penance. In defence of Herbert, who was a holy and generous man in an age of greed and crime, it must be said that the tale was first told by the canons of the cathedral. They had reason to dislike him for, following Norman policy, he had replaced the chapter of canons who had ministered in the cathedral by Benedictine monks. There were to be no more secular canons here until Henry VIII again refounded the chapter.

Herbert laid the cathedral's foundation stone in 1096, and through his energy and personal generosity the work was so far advanced that its first Consecration took place on 24th September 1101. This is the more remarkable, in that he was also building two of England's largest priory-cum-parish churches: St. Nicholas', at Yarmouth, and at St. Margaret's, Lynn. It seems that the whole ground plan was determined from the first, and that portions of the building were pressed forward so rapidly that the native builders were encouraged to follow their own methods, for the west wall of the cloister is of pre-Conquest style, with its small Saxon double-splayed circular windows. The site was already holy ground, for beneath the modern St. Saviour's Chapel at the east end are the foundations of a pre-Conquest chapel, partly re-used as foundations for the Norman chapel formerly there; there are also indications of a Saxon cemetery nearby.

Before Herbert's death in 1119, he had probably completed the presbytery with its chapels, the transepts, and four bays of the nave. The speed with which the work progressed strikingly demonstrates the vigour of the race of men who built it. The Normans possessed the energy and immaturity of a young race. But a few years before they had been wild pagans, roving the seas, and conquering new lands over a wide area. They embraced their new faith with equal ardour, and enriched their conquered territories with great churches. Yet their architecture was not as yet forward-looking. They copied the architecture of such Roman buildings as were still standing, so that each side of Norwich nave looks like the Coliseum unrolled, or like an aqueduct. Their virility was showing itself in the richness and vigour of their sculpture, but the

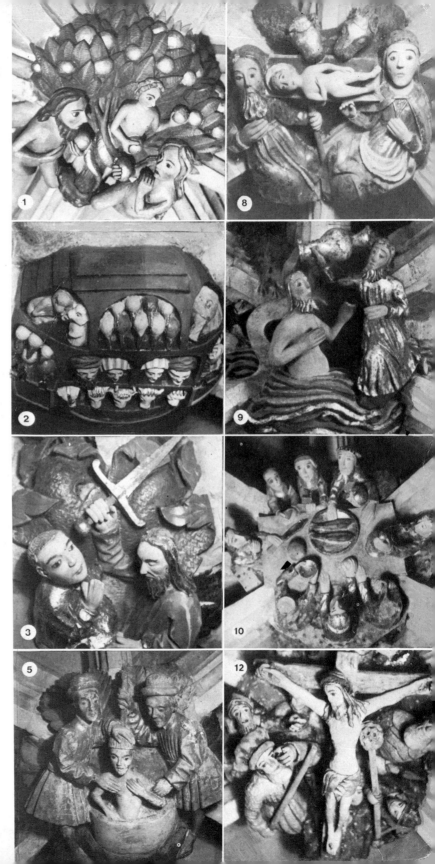

pointed arch, with the inspired revolution known today as Gothic architecture, was still a thing of the future when the walls of Norwich Cathedral were finished.

The Norman ground plan, which still remains less altered than in any other English cathedral, was typical of its period, with certain local features, such as the very long nave, comparing with those of the neighbouring Ely, Peterborough, and St. Albans, and contrasting with the shorter naves of Durham, Chichester, and Gloucester. The high triforium, as high as the side aisles beneath it, compares with our nearer neighbours, whilst it contrasts with the high aisles and low triforia of other districts. A luxurious feature, still rare in 1101, is the ambulatory or aisle right round the apse, permitting processions to go behind the High Altar.

Herbert de Losinga died on 22nd July 1119, and was buried before the High Altar of his cathedral church.

His successor, Everard de Montgomery, was enthroned in 1121. It seems likely that the Ancient Throne was brought from Thetford and set up here in time for that event.

Everard appears to have completed the cathedral to the west end and the roof by about 1145. The Norman cloisters and monastic buildings, including the refectory, much of which survives today, were being built about the same time. The tower, the highest Norman tower in England, was probably completed to the level of its interior ceiling by Everard, and finished to the base of the battlements by his successor, William de Turbe, about 1170. It would at first have been crowned by a low timber or possibly stone spire like those in the Rhineland.

So far, we have described the church mainly as that of the bishops, whose seat gives the building its title cathedral (from *kathedra*, Greek for seat or throne—compare the Portuguese title *Sé*—the church of the *Sedes* or Seat of the Bishop). The diocesan mother church is also of necessity a collegiate church, i.e. one whose life and worship are maintained by a college or collection of people. In England in the early missionary days the college usually took the form of a *Minster*, not a monastery but a group of mission priests travelling over a wide area but centring their life on the mother church. Later the college would take the form of a group of *canons* (men who live by a rule of life, from the Greek *kanon* or rule); St. Paul's, York, Lichfield, Hereford, Lincoln, Chichester, Salisbury, Exeter and Wells have survived to this day with this form unchanged and are therefore known as cathedrals of the Old Foundation.

Other cathedrals, of which Norwich is one, are of the New Foundation, i.e. they were re-founded by Henry VIII as a dean and chapter modelled in general on the Old Foundations, but from the time of the Norman Conquest (or before) to the Dissolu-

*Continued on page 10*

*   *   *

LEFT: *The transepts, looking north. The roof bosses illustrate: north transept, Jesus' childhood and the Blessed Virgin's life; south transept, Jesus' ministry.*

RIGHT: *The nave, looking west. Bishop Lyhart's west window and vaulted roof (1470) fit surprisingly well on to the Norman walls.*

tion of the Monasteries (about 1538), they were staffed by a monastery, generally of the Order of St. Benedict.

The monks' first duty, as with all clergy, was the *Opus Dei* or Work of God, i.e. worship. The form of worship at Norwich Cathedral followed the Sarum Use (for it was only one or two *secular* cathedrals, i.e. with canons instead of monks, who had their own independent Use). Within the Sarum Use, Norwich had, like most great churches, its own local customs. Evidence for these is provided by the *Consuetudinarium Ecclesie Norwyc*, now in the library of Corpus Christi College, Cambridge*. This includes

festivals such as St. Felix on 8th March, Little St. William (a child wrongly supposed to have been crucified by Jews) on 24th March, St. Ethelbert King and Martyr on 20th May, and the cathedral Dedication Festival on 24th September. Other local customs include placing lights in the triforia, both upper and lower, on great feasts.

The impression made on Europe by the monastic orders is perhaps greater than that of any other institution, except perhaps the Roman Empire. To take one aspect alone—their planning—one can go from Cyprus to Sweden, from Portugal to Scotland, and find that the planning

of the cloister and its surrounding buildings is in general similar. You can take the "Visitors' Guide to Norwich Cathedral" on the inside front cover of this book, and with it, guide yourself round an average monastery in any European land, and see where the brethren worshipped, ate, slept, worked—and where many do so today. Perhaps nothing but Roman roads and ruins gives Europe such a sense of unity.

Norwich Cathedral Priory is of outstanding interest, because of the unusually clear evidence it provides of the life lived within it from the twelfth to the sixteenth century. Its activities are recorded in detail in a series of over 3,500 rolls, which, with many other documents extending from 1272 (when previous ones were burnt) to the Dissolution, form the most complete and best preserved collection in England**. Its title Priory, rather than Abbey, implies that the real head of the community in a monastic cathedral was the prior (or *First* member), for the bishop, corresponding with the abbot, was mainly occupied with the diocese.

The monks numbered sixty until the gradual decline following the Black Death, and there were besides many clerks, squires, and general servants, forming a great and well organised community. Abundant hospitality to rich and poor was an important activity. Maintenance of the Community's wide activities cost

*Continued on page 14*

*

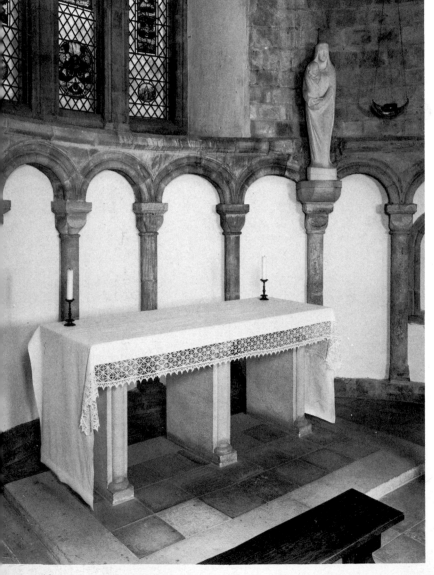

LEFT: *St. Andrew's Chapel adjoining the north transept. Fine Norman work. The window is a thirteenth-century insertion. The glass, sixteenth- and seventeenth-century, is from the Deanery. Arms: Mayor Ramsey, Henry VIII, Wolsey, Nykke (outer lights); Deans Suckling, Montgomery, and Gardiner (centre lights).*

RIGHT: *The Reliquary Arch houses the Treasury given by the Worshipful Company of Goldsmiths of London in 1972. It was built about 1424 to house relics and to form an ante-chapel to the nearby Reliquary Chapel (now destroyed). Early fourteenth-century paintings in vault.*

* "Norwich Cathedral Priory Customary", J. B. L. Tolhurst, Henry Bradshaw Society, Vol. LXXXII.

** "An Introduction to the Rolls of Norwich Cathedral Priory", by Dr. H. W. Saunders.

RIGHT: *England's finest Norman apse, surmounted with a later clerestory and vault which enable it to compare with the great apses of the continent. Golden* wells, a rebus or pun on the name of its builder, Goldwell, embellish the bosses of the vault.
ABOVE: *The Erpingham window in the* presbytery north aisle. *A fine collection of medieval Norwich glass from various donors and sources assembled and leaded by Kings of Norwich in 1963.*

£2,500 a year—well over £100,000 of our money.

Amongst the monks, twelve had special duties. The Master of the Cellar, an office peculiar to Norwich, had a varied responsibility including entertainment of guests and wide activities outside; he had a staff of fifty. The cellarer fed the community; his large staff included a curer of herrings, which presumably came from Yarmouth whose prior had his special lodging in the cloister, next to that of the prior of Lynn; food included 10,000 eggs a week. The sacrist maintained the furnishings of worship; he used eleven hundredweight of wool annually, and bought cloths from as far apart as Antioch and Aylsham. The precentor led the services and cared for the music and its books. The chamberlain arranged all the clothing on the widest scale. The almoner distributed to the poor, including prisoners, lepers, and the grammar school boys (not, of course, the grammar school as re-founded by Edward VI); he gave out 10,000 loaves of bread a year. The hostiliar was over the guest hall; the refectorer supervised the refectory or dining hall, and the infirmar maintained the infirmary where the sick monks lay. His purchases included nutmegs, saffron, poppy, fennel, grains of paradise, dyeaquilon, and libanus. The pittancer and communar provided extra allowances of food and drink for feast days. But the monks voluntarily went without these for long periods, to find money to rebuild the cloister, and we must now turn to this, one of the finest cloisters in the world.

Of the Norman cloister there remain the surrounding walls, with, on the south side, considerable remains of the refectory, whose northward

*

LEFT: *A close-up view of the sanctuary and the Bishop's throne. As a place of Christian worship this is the most interesting sanctuary in England; it preserves the plan universal from early days to 1100, superseded thereafter for 850 years, and now being revived by the Liturgical Movement. This is recovering the New Testament simplicity of family worship round the Lord's Table. The custom of celebrating Holy Communion facing the people, for which such a sanctuary was intended, has remained in use in some places, notably the Papal altar in St. Peter's, Rome. It is normal among the Free Churches and is being widely revived today.*

windows have since oddly become the southward windows of the library. Judging by the remains preserved in the cathedral, the cloister walks would have resembled such contemporary cloisters as Monreale in Sicily, and St. Paul's, Rome, with small round-arched openings resting on pairs of pilasters.

Then came the riot of 1272, when the citizens burnt the cloisters and did much other damage, so much that the church had to be re-consecrated on Advent Sunday 1278, in the presence of King Edward I and Queen Eleanor.

A great scheme of rebuilding the destroyed monastic buildings began between 1289 and 1299 with the chapter house, of which only the foundations survive. The rebuilding of the cloister walks was begun in 1297 and not finished until 1430. Most of it was paid for by the priory, through the monks' sacrifice of their extra allowances on feast days. First the three bays opposite the arches leading to the chapter house were rebuilt, then those to the northward leading to the church, then the remainder of the east walk, then between 1318 and 1330 the south walk. The west walk was begun in 1338 and carried on until the Black Death put a stop to all building. Little more was done until about 1410, when the north walk was begun; this was completed about 1430.

The cloisters possess many features of great interest. Walking round them from their eastern entrance from the church, we see evidence of their former use. The entrance itself, one of the finest Gothic doorways in England, is called "The Prior's Door", from the mitred head of Henry de Lakenham, prior 1287–1311, which appears above it. Proceeding along the east walk, we see, in order, book cupboards, some still usable, many blocked; on the stone seat indications of games once played there; next the blocked entrance to the parlour (the talking place—from *parler*) or trea-saunce; then the three arches once leading to the chapter house where

*

daily business was done. Next is the blocked entrance to the dormitory, the door was double, and usually only half opened, as one side only of the step is worn; beyond is the blocked entrance to the former warming house, with the monastery's only fire, beside that of the kitchen. In the south walk are, first the dark entry, formerly

leading to the infirmary and prior's hall; beyond these were the granary, the brewery, the water gate now known as Pull's Ferry, whence the stone was brought for the building, and the city. Then a small door which today leads to the library; next, the large door formerly leading to the refectory and kitchen. In the west

15

walk are, the lavatory (*lavo*, "I wash"), with the gulley for water, and arches above for towels; next the guest house doorway, with, above, a boss representing the ever-open door; lastly the door to the locutorium (*loquor*, "I talk"), where visitors were interviewed; this is today the visitors' gift shop, and St. Christopher, carved above it, has become especially appropriate. In the north walk are the

*

ABOVE: *Medieval Norwich painters produced work comparable with that of Italy. These panels in St. Saviour's Chapel (the chapel of the Royal Norfolk Regiment) came from St. Michael-at-Plea Church. When rector there, the author arranged for their restoration, for which the Pilgrim Trust paid £1,000. The Royal Norfolk Regiment had the panels framed in 1958, and in 1963 erected the collegiate stalls as a memorial to the officers, men and achievements of the Regiment.*

two entrances to the church, of which the western one is called "The Monks' Door".

Returning to the earliest part of the cloister, we study the bosses in the vaulted roof. These form an unrivalled collection. The earliest show leaf forms, oak, hawthorn, wild rose, and grape. From here to the Prior's Door are incidents from the Passion, with the four Evangelists against the east wall. Then, starting from the dark entry and finishing by the locutory door, is a series of a hundred from the Book of Revelation, perhaps the finest series of its kind in the world. They resemble manuscript illuminations of the period, and are easy to identify with the Book of Revelation in one's hand. Subjects include God enthroned, angels and kings worshipping Him, the Lamb slain and triumphant being worshipped, the heavenly orchestra with medieval instruments, the opening of the Seven Seals, the Seven

Trumpets, the Four Horsemen, the Seven Vials, the Fall of Babylon, and the Last Judgment. Many other subjects appear also, including a fourteenth-century windmill at work, the Trinity, and lives of saints. Some amongst many in the north walk, starting from the east, are New Testament incidents from the Resurrection onwards, events such as the Martyrdoms of St. Edmund and St. Thomas of Canterbury, Henry II doing penance for this, and a charter being presented to a monastery.

*Continued on page 18*

*

RIGHT: *These panels (top), in the exhibition in the Visitors' Centre, came from St. Michael-at-Plea. The Betrayal and Crucifixion formed part of a retable, c. 1385. The retable (below) is said to have been given by Bishop Despenser and others about 1381. It was restored and placed in St. Luke's Chapel in 1958.*

Architecturally the cloisters are of great interest. The uniformity of their general shape is remarkable for work spread over so long a period. The development of details such as the window tracery proceeds from Geometrical in the early bays, through the Flowing Decorated of rich early fourteenth-century England, coming to a sudden stop with two bays where the tracery appears to be a temporary substitute in oak which has never been replaced. Finally there is Perpendicular, the economy measure used after the Black Death. Though to the untrained eye the vaulting ribs appear similar throughout, they show a subtle development. Above is the unusual upper storey, perhaps built for winter use. The form of the cloister originated in the sunny south of Europe, with the courtyard or patio which was admirably adapted for finding shade in a hot climate. It was unsuited to the cold north, yet it was long before men

learnt to glaze it, as at Gloucester Cathedral. The upper storey is used today for storage of documents, the library, and the old choristers' rooms, whilst the cloister itself is sometimes used for tea parties in connection with cathedral services.

Returning to the church, we continue the tale of its building. The only large additions made at ground level to the Norman building were the Lady Chapel, 1245–1257, and St. Anne's Chapel, both destroyed, and the Bauchon Chapel of our Lady of Pity, built about 1330 and restored as the Chapel of the Friends of the Cathedral, 1968, whilst St. Saviour's Chapel, designed by Sir Charles Nicholson and built in 1930, stands on the site of the Norman St. Saviour's and the later Lady Chapel. The Saxon foundations were discovered on digging its foundations.

A disastrous gale in 1362 brought down the spire. In its fall it destroyed

the Norman clerestory of the apse. Thomas Percy, bishop 1355–69, brother of the Earl of Northumberland, rebuilt the clerestory on its present splendid scale, giving England the only truly English apse which can rival those of France (Westminster Abbey apse is itself a French design). Though only 85 feet high, little more than half the height of Beauvais Cathedral vault, it can stand comparison with its continental rivals because of its perfect proportions. Percy covered it with a timber roof. The nave and transepts were still roofed only with timber, which led to disastrous fires.

The Normans were on the whole poor engineers. Too many of their buildings collapsed. In particular they felt unable to vault their high roofs in stone. Knowing only the semi-circular arch, they were forced to design areas which they wished to vault in a series of squares, for a square is the only shape which can be covered with a vault of intersecting *semi-circular* arches. So Norwich side aisles were vaulted by the Normans in a series of squares. Every second pair of pillars in the nave is larger than the intervening pair, dividing the nave into a series of large squares, giving the impression that the Normans contemplated an intersecting vault like those in the Angevin area of France, where each bay of vaulting covers a square area. But this idea was not carried out.

*Continued on page 20*

★

RIGHT: *The Bauchon Chapel, south of the presbytery, was restored as the Chapel of the Friends of Norwich Cathedral in 1968. The statue, by Mr. John Skelton, shows Our Lady as representing dignified modern womanhood. The seat front is medieval. Glass, by Moria Forsyth, 1964, shows members of the Benedictine order. Iron screen, modern. Crucifixion shows Byzantine "Christ in Glory". Picture by Opie.*

LEFT: *The bosses in the Bauchon Chapel roof illustrate a tale of an empress falsely accused by her brother who had tried to seduce her, but was saved by the Virgin. Centre row (south to north): 1. The emperor, empress and brother. 2. Empress heals brother on condition he confesses guilt. 3. Blessed Virgin in glory. 4. Empress kneels before returning emperor. 5. Brother murders child whom empress is nursing, puts dagger into her hand whilst asleep, and thus fixes blame on her.*

The present choir stalls, no doubt replacing earlier ones, were constructed about 1420 by John Wakering, bishop 1416–25, whose arms are recalled by the hawks on some of the canopies*. The misericordes are very fine. Then came the great fire of 1463, caused by lightning striking the spire. The nave roof was burnt, and those stalls which stood under the tower were destroyed. They were reconstructed, with canopies of a different design extending across the transepts, about 1480. Later some more reconstruction was done to them about 1515, after the fire of 1509, in the transepts.

The fire of 1463 necessitated a far greater work—structurally perhaps our finest achievement—the stone vaulting of the nave, carried out by Walter Lyhart, bishop 1446–72. This is a lierne vault, i.e. the main ribs are joined by small ribs crossing from one to another. The bosses at the intersection of the ribs form an exceptionally fine series. From the tower westward they illustrate the Old Testament from Creation to King Solomon, thence the New Testament, to the Last Judgment at the west end.

* See "The Stalls of Norwich Cathedral" by A. B. Whittingham.

Lyhart also constructed the pulpitum or screen between the nave and choir. The Bauchon Chapel had been vaulted about 1450.

James Goldwell, bishop 1472–99, erected the vault of the presbytery, together with the flying buttresses outside, to support it. He also built the present stone spire, 315 feet high, the second highest in England. Richard Nykke, bishop 1501–36, completed the vaulting by erecting the transept vaults.

The Dissolution of the Monasteries in 1538 saw changes, but also here a surprising degree of continuity. The last prior, William Castleton, became the first dean, the monks became canons or minor canons, the offices of organist, precentor, sacrist, singing man, and chorister remained, and all these continue today. The Statutes of the New Foundation even provided "The Common Table of the Ministers", i.e. the monastic refectory continuing in use like a college dining hall. Perhaps the most striking example of continuity was Osbert Parsley. As his monument in the nave states, he became a singing man or lay clerk in the choir in 1535, singing the Latin services; he maintained his position through the Dissolution, the

reigns of Edward VI and Mary, and survived through Elizabeth's reign until 1585.

Continuity with the old order is preserved in the office of the Bishop of Norwich in a unique manner. When Henry VIII was dissolving the greater monasteries, he found that the bishop's income would provide him more money than that of St. Benet's Abbey nearby. He therefore appropriated the episcopal endowments, substituted for them the revenues of St. Benet's, and made William Rugg, the last abbot of

*Continued on page 22*

*

ABOVE: *This is unique amongst English episcopal effigies as it represents Bishop Goldwell in cope instead of chasuble over eucharistic vestments, as he would appear during a solemn service such as the consecration of a church.*

RIGHT: *The ambulatory. Note the perspectives of arches and vaulting and the elegant "Early English" arches, of 1250, once leading to the Lady Chapel of that date. The sixteenth-century window shows St. Bryce, Bishop of Tours, 397–444, holding live coals in his cope, thus testifying his innocence of an accusation. The fifteenth-century seven sacrament font in nearby St. Luke's Chapel came from the ruined church of St. Mary-in-the-Marsh about 1570.*

St. Benet's, bishop of Norwich in 1536. St. Benet's Abbey has never been dissolved, and the bishop of Norwich remains as the one mitred abbot of the old order in England.

The English Prayer Book provided simpler services and ritual. But during the last four centuries, church music has advanced by steps in their way as impressive as the development of architecture in earlier days. The Statutes of the New Foundation at Norwich provided for six minor canons to sing the services, eight lay clerks "to be expert in singing", an organist, and eight choristers. No doubt they eagerly acquired and sang the music of each great new composer as he came to be known—Byrd, Morley (who may have worked here for a time), Weelkes, Orlando Gibbons, and the rest.

As everywhere in England, there was a sad break in the continuity of Church life during the Rebellion of the seventeenth century. Joseph Hall, bishop 1641–56, suffered the loss of his property, whilst his description of the sacrilege committed in the cathedral in 1643 has often been quoted. But the cathedral recovered its life speedily at the Restoration. The City Corporation gave the candlesticks on the High Altar; a new organ, parts of which still exist, was erected on the pulpitum, and music recovered its old standard—soon to be enriched by the work of the new composers, Purcell and his successors, and despite the ineptitude of leaders appointed in the eighteenth and early nineteenth centuries, the cathedral's life continued to develop.

*Continued on page 24*

\*

RIGHT: *The Cloister was built to be full of life—a life which influenced early medieval England as profoundly as her universities today. Before the invention of printing, one walk was the scriptorium, or place where monks worked copying books by hand, often illuminating them in gold and colours.*

LEFT: *Examples of roof bosses in the Cloisters. East Walk: 1, Harrowing of Hell (I Peter 3; 19). 2, Crucifixion. South Walk: 3, The Son of Man (Rev. 1; 13). 4, Adoration of the Lamb (Rev. 5; 6). West Walk: 5, Fall of Babylon (Rev. 16; 19). North Walk: 6, King Edmund's martyrdom at Hoxne. 7, Martyrdom of St. Thomas of Canterbury. 8, Henry II's penance at St. Thomas's tomb.*

During the modern revival of Church life, the cathedral has been restored and adapted to modern use, and its standard of worship and music greatly improved. It has become truly the Mother Church of its Diocese and justifies its life more strikingly than ever before. Modern transport brings visitors from everywhere and its nave is frequently crowded for special events. Its choir sings superbly and radio and television bring its services into every home. Anyone can gain an intimate relationship with it by joining its "Friends". Its treasures are well cared for and new treasures are often given.

Alan Webster, Dean from 1970 to 1978, installed above the western cloister a Visitors' Centre, Coffee and Refreshment Room, Exhibition and Tape/Slide Theatre, showing a guide to the cathedral with its music and a tape for the under-tens, entered by steps adjoining the cathedral shop. In the Exhibition are models of the monastery and ships bringing stone from Caen, manuscripts and alabaster, highlighting medieval ideas of God, Julian of Norwich's insights, and faith's problems and possibilities today when scientific discovery and the theories of Darwin, Marx and Freud question old views. Our search for God is seen in photographs of moments of joy in life and in the work of Mother Teresa of Calcutta.

Five hundred volunteers help here each month. The cathedral is also a momentary monastery for pilgrims. As centre of a community concerned with service, human and divine, it means more, to more people, than ever before, and it witnesses today to God's power and peace in a world of weakness and strife.

★

ABOVE LEFT: *The Erpingham Gate. Built in 1420, this was the public entrance leading directly to the cathedral, whilst the Ethelbert Gate, to the south, led to the monastery.*

LEFT: *Norwich Cathedral Visitors' Centre, Coffee Room and Exhibition, opened by The Queen in 1975, showing a model and some original stones.*

*The photographs in this book are by the following: Angelo Hornak: pp. 5, 6 (top), 8, 9, 10, 13, 14, 21; Gerald Newbery, F.I.I.P., F.R.P.S.: pp. 1, 6 (centre and bottom), 12, 15, 18, 24, back cover; C. J. Nicholas, A.I.I.P.: pp. 2, 4, 11, 16, 17, 20, 23; A. E. Coe & Sons Ltd.: front cover, pp. 3, 19; E. C. Le Grice, F.R.P.S.: pp. 7, 22.*

SBN 85372 105 X